1

IT ALL BEGAN

WITH A NUMBER 2

LEAD PENCIL

SECOND EDITION

It All Began With a Number Two Lead Pencil

Second Edition

By Diane Coleman

Copyright ©2018, 2022 by George Parmer

Requests for information should be sent to:

Susan R. Kent

Susan.Kent@rwcwarranty.com

Cover design: Denise McGurl

Design and production: Nat Belz, Books Brothers

Printed in the United States of America

V2.0 ISBN 9798829960629

BOOKS BROTHERS PRESS
15 WESTCHESTER DRIVE
ASHEVILLE, NC 28803

FOREWORD

As I write this foreword, I reflect back to the first "It all began with a #2 lead pencil" book written 16 years ago. I reflect on what has happened in that period of time and how God has continued his blessing on my family and the associates and people in our company.

As I write this foreword and think about the blessings, there are so many that I will not be able to capture all of them. My love for Barbara grows more and more each year, our daughter Eve and our son Adam have grown up and now have families within walking distance from our home. As grandparents that is a huge blessing. To see Adam and Eve living in a godly way and bringing up their children in that way as well is another huge blessing. Our other two children have lived most of their lives away from us. We continue to pray for them as we do not see them as often as we would like.

I still from time to time think of our parents who are home with The Lord and two sisters who now do not live as close as we would like. The path of life was built from the love our family had. My mother was always loving and caring and now I see that same trait in the daily walk of Adam and Eve. I know that many years from now we will all be together in eternity with our Heavenly Father. That thought is one that helps when we have situations that happen that are not pleasant.

When my sisters and I were young, we just did not know how financially poor we were. Looking back in 2002 and still looking back today I realize that we were never poor in love. We had our mother along with a father who covered all things with love. When I think of our mother, I always go to God's word, First Corinthians 13, which tells us.

> If I speak in the tongues[a] of men or of angels, but do not have love, I am only a resounding gong or a clanging cymbal. [2] If I have the gift of prophecy and can fathom all mysteries and all knowledge, and if I have a faith that can move mountains, but do not have love, I am nothing. [3] If I give all I possess to the poor and give over my body to hardship that I may boast,[b] but do not have love, I gain nothing.

> [4] Love is patient, love is kind. It does not envy, it does not boast, it is not proud. [5] It does not dishonor others, it is not self-seeking, it is not easily angered, it keeps no record of wrongs. [6] Love does not delight in evil but rejoices with the truth. [7] It always protects, always trusts, always hopes, always perseveres.

> [8] Love never fails. But where there are prophecies, they will cease; where there are tongues, they will be stilled; where there is knowledge, it will pass away. [9] For we know in part and we prophesy in part, [10] but when completeness comes, what is in part disappears. [11] When I was a child, I talked like a child, I thought like a child, I reasoned like a child. When I became a man, I put the ways of childhood behind me. [12] For now we see only a reflection as in a mirror; then we shall see face to face. Now I know in part; then I shall know fully, even as I am fully known.

> [13] And now these three remain: faith, hope and love. But the greatest of these is love.

I am also grateful and thankful for the blessings of the associates and people of all our companies. I cannot put into words and express my thankfulness for such a dedicated, honest and caring group of people. I would like to single out names, but will not do so because I might miss naming someone who contributed to my success. I simply say "thanks" to each and every one of you for who you are and what you did day in and day out. You all know who I'm referring to, because of the size the companies have grown to I find it hard to not get around to thank each and every one of you for your labors on behalf of the companies. My thanks and gratitude to each and every one of you.

To Diane Coleman, who 16 years ago wrote the first book and now has graciously taken the time to write this book. I know the research and time she took was truly outstanding—thank you, Diane.

In my book 16 years ago I was approaching the "late fall or winter" of my life. Now approaching my 79th year I stop and reflect the love of our Heavenly Father and what he has done by sending his only son Jesus to bear the sins of his children. I think I'm more adamant in my concern that all people I know come to the saving knowledge of Jesus Christ. It is so simple to trust and accept this gift of salvation. Repent and confess your sins to God and pray the sinner's prayer (example below). If you have not done this I would ask that you consider doing so before you go to sleep tonight.

God tells us in His word that the only way to heaven is through His Son, the Lord Jesus Christ. When I came to know this, I did not know how to do it. When I found out how simple it was, I was overjoyed by the truth of God's Holy Word! For anyone who feels God tugging on your heart and wants to come to this saving knowledge and accept Jesus as your personal Savior and Lord, all you have to do is pray this prayer:

"Confessing to God that I am a sinner, and believing that The Lord Jesus Christ dies for my sins on the cross and was raised for my justification, I do now receive and confess Him as my personal Savior."

If you are sincere in this prayer (and the Almighty will know!), you will be regenerated by the Holy Spirit, and your life will be changed!

George Parmer, April 2022

TAKE ME OUT
TO THE BALL GAME

"It's a beautiful day at Shibe Park!" Baseball announcer Al Helfer's voice pierced through the static of the tabletop radio in the parlor of a simple wooden frame house in rural Northumberland County, PA. It was June 11, 1950.

George Parmer Sr.'s[1] favorite team, the Philadelphia Athletics, was hosting the Cleveland Indians. He had been looking forward to the game all week. His ten-year-old son, also named George, sat cross-legged on a well-worn living room rug.

"Brilliant blue sky and white fleecy clouds, with wind from behind left center field," Helfer continued. A slight breeze ruffled the curtains at the window and George Jr. imagined it was the same air that wafted over A's pitcher Bobby Shantz. "Old Shandy" was a left-hander and "a little guy," commented Helfer, "...150 lbs. with his spikes on and completely soaking wet!" Both Georges chuckled.

An old diesel truck rumbled along the road in front of the house and George Jr. turned up the radio. It was 88-year-

---

1   The two Georges did not share a middle name, but the terms "Sr." and "Jr." will be used in these early chapters to avoid confusion.

old Connie Mack's 50th and last season as A's manager, his Golden Jubilee as "The Grand Old Man of Baseball" and young George wanted to make sure he heard every word. As the veteran sportscasters called out the play-by-play, George Sr. watched his enthusiastic son with amusement.

By the end of the third inning, Cleveland was ahead 3-2. Innings four through six limped by, scoreless. At the bottom of the seventh, A's pitcher Shantz sacrificed to move catcher Joe Astroth to second base. Then Cleveland's pitcher Jim Lemon walked third baseman Bob Dillinger to first. When right-fielder Wally Moses approached the plate, the crowd felt the change in momentum. Fans began clapping in rhythm to "get the A's going."

It worked. Moses hit a fly ball into right field. Cleveland's Bob Kennedy couldn't get to it in time. Astroth ran home and the game was tied, 3-3. The bases were loaded, with only one out. The crowd went wild.

So did the two Georges. "Lemon has his work cut out for him," commented announcer Art Gleason. Center-fielder Sam Chapman approached the plate. But the A's rally was not to be. Both Chapman and first baseman Ferris Fain were called out, one on a fly catch and the other tagged at first. The three players stranded on base dejectedly trotted back to the dugout.

The disappointed Georges reminded themselves that there were two more innings to play. It was "one of those ball games where it could jump either way," Al Helfer reminded his audience.

And jump it did. Innings eight and nine remained scoreless and the game went into extra innings. The Indians caught fire in the top of the tenth. Catcher Jim Hegan hit an almost effortless home run, as if he had just casually "slapped at that ball," said Helfer. Hegan, Al Rosen and Lou Boudreau all crossed the plate, extending the Indians' lead to 6-3.

Al Helfer remarked diplomatically that "anything can happen in a ball game, you know" as the A's came up to bat. With two outs, Mack sent in pinch hitter Barney McCoskey at the end of the inning. But he couldn't get it done. The game whimpered to a sad close for the Georges' beloved A's.

George Jr. flopped down on the rug, flinging his arms out to his sides, exhausted. His father shook his head. There was no need for words.

Words weren't necessary anyway. Young George's wild gesturing was not a result of excess energy or unbridled excitement. For three hours, he had communicated every play of the game to his father in American Sign Language.

George Sr. was totally deaf.

CHAPTER ONE

George John Parmer and Mabel Margaret Seaman met in the 1920s when they were both students at the Germantown School for the Deaf in Philadelphia. Crockery-maker David G. Seixas established the school in the early 1800s, housing the students in his own home and providing food, clothing, and schooling at his own expense. When the number of children outgrew the space, he moved the facility to the southeast corner of 11th and High Streets.

By 1821, a group of prominent citizens joined Seixas' effort. They incorporated The Pennsylvania Institution for the Deaf and Dumb [Mute] as a charitable society. On February 8, 1821, the Pennsylvania General Assembly recognized the school as "an asylum and school in the city of Philadelphia, where the children of the rich, for a moderate compensation, and of the poor, gratuitously, laboring under the privation of the faculty of speech, are maintained and educated." The school had a religious underpinning; its first president was Episcopal Bishop William White.

In 1826, the society erected a fine new building on the corner of Broad and Pine Street. The Greek revival structure was designed by John Haviland, William Strickland, and Frank Furness, three of America's most notable 19th century architects. In 1892-23, the school moved again, this time to a 70-acre campus in the Mount Airy neighborhood of Philadelphia. It remained there until 1984.[2]

Despite its noble cause and stellar reputation, the school was not without controversy. According to Henri Gaillard, in the book *Gaillard in Deaf America: A Portrait of the Deaf Community, 1917*:

"[By 1892] the Mr. Airy campus earned national notice. Sign language, its headmaster Albert Crouter declared, was an unnecessary and unwanted reminder of a past era. Under his leadership, the school was divided into two distinct groups: the first for the majority of students to be taught in a pure oral environment; the second for 'oral failures,' to be instructed in sign language. By 1899, ninety percent of students were raised in an all-oral environment.

"Not surprisingly, deaf educators and leaders in Pennsylvania and across the country challenged Crouter's claims. In one critique, several advocates charged that students who did not acquire oral skills were often mislabeled 'feeble-minded' and improperly dismissed. Without the power to investigate the school, these critics were unable to alter the practices they decried."[3]

At the time George Sr. and Mabel attended, the school had over 500 students, divided almost evenly between boys and girls. Most of the students received financial assistance through the commonwealth of Pennsylvania or foundation

---

2   The school is now located in the Germantown section of Philadelphia and continues to serve hearing-impaired students from preschool through high school. It is one of four state-chartered schools currently serving this population.

3   Gaillard, Henri, and Robert M. Buchanan. 2002. Gaillard in Deaf America : A Portrait of the Deaf Community, 1917 / Henri Gaillard ; Bob Buchanan, editor ; translated by William Sayers. Gallaudet classics in deaf studies. Washington, D.C.: Gallaudet University Press. p. 10.

grants. A few came from neighboring home states.

Although the oral method was emphasized, all of the students eventually became prolific signers. Gaillard also notes, "In addition to the classics, the pupils read a large number of magazines, scientific or literary journals, even daily newspapers. It is reading, and this cannot be stressed too much, that enhances the knowledge of the deaf. And by permitting its pupils to read general publications, Mount Airy, like other American institutions, advances their knowledge of life and its problems."[4]

In addition to general education, the school offered a wide variety of vocational training options, including home economics, masonry, cabinetry and furniture repair, dressmaking and tailoring, printing, shoemaking, and gardening. George and Mabel studied several of these disciplines during high school.

The students of the school wrote and published a periodical called "Mt. Airy World," containing essays "about pupils and their doings, and articles in defense of the deaf. 'The deaf are not defectives,'"[5] it declared, championing the wide-ranging abilities and potential of the school's graduates.

George Sr. and Mabel received an excellent education and exemplified the school's "can-do" spirit. They married after graduation in the late '20s and set up housekeeping in a rented home in the tiny town of Marietta in Lancast-

---

4   Ibid. p. 134
5   Ibid. p. 135. During this time in history, any disability was a definite handicap to functioning within our culture. The Americans with Disabilities Act, designed to alleviate this inequality, would not be signed into law until 1990.

er County, PA. George found janitorial work in Harrisburg, 30 miles away. He stayed in a local boarding home during the week and returned to Marietta every weekend. Within a few years, they started a family. Delores was born in 1930 and Jean in 1934. George Aldus came along during a thunderstorm on a very hot and humid August 24, 1939.

The little family was doing fine until mid-1940s when the railroad, king of mass transportation at the time, developed plans to build a new line through Lancaster County. The tracks ran directly through George and Mabel's rental home. The railroad had secured the property rights from the owner and the Parmers had no choice but to move.

They had to do it quickly. Government agents only gave them three days to vacate the house. To make matters worse, they served notice to Mabel on a weekday when George was still in Harrisburg. She had to figure out how to move the family without her husband's help, with American Sign Language as her only means of communication. George Jr. was only a year old at the time.

Rental houses were almost impossible to secure at short notice, so they moved to Mabel's father's farm in rural northern Dauphin County where the commute time to Harrisburg would be about the same for George Sr.

Living in the country had its perks for the young family. In Marietta, Mabel had used canned milk because she did not have a refrigerator. But on the farm the children had sweet milk right from the cow, chilled in a metal milk can immersed in the ice-cold water that flowed under the spring house. One of young George's earliest memories is his grandfather giving him fresh whole milk one early morning. It made a big impression. For over 75 years George has shared that memory with deep fondness toward his grandfather who saved him from the dreaded canned milk.

The Parmer family moved twice more, finally settling into a modest frame house on Mahantango Creek Road in Northumberland County. No electricity, no bathroom, no exterior paint. A coal stove in the kitchen was the only source of heat for the entire house. Mabel sent the children off to bed every winter night with heating irons tucked in beside them.

The Parmers were one of the poorest families in the valley, often borrowing money to buy coal for that stove. But their young children were unaware of the family's financial struggles. Their parents were fun-loving and affectionate. Mabel frequently set aside her chores to play with the children, lining up chairs to play train or joining them in a favorite game. Recalls George, "She had a 'First Corinthians 13 heart."[6]

By the early 1940s the United States was engaged in World War II and many essential commodities were scarce or unavailable. "Most families were allocated 3 US gallons of gasoline a week, which sharply curtailed driving for any purpose. Production of most durable goods, like cars, new housing, vacuum cleaners, and kitchen appliances, was banned until the war ended. Gasoline, meat, and clothing were tightly rationed."[7]

---

6   Verses 4-7 state: "Love is patient and kind; love does not envy or boast; it is not arrogant or rude. It does not insist on its own way; it is not irritable or resentful; it does not rejoice at wrongdoing, but rejoices with the truth. Love bears all things, believes all things, hopes all things, endures all things."

7   https://en.wikipedia.org/wiki/United_States_home_front_during_World_War_II

As a result, the Parmer family had to make do with limited bread, shoes ("only two pairs per year," Jean recalls), and many other important items. Manufacturing plants that originally made appliances and vehicles now turned out war equipment and military gear. When Mabel signed up to buy a refrigerator, she realized with chagrin that she was at the end of a waiting list of over 100 people.

School-aged children joined the work force to help supplement family incomes. Young George and his friends spent most of their out-of-school time in the local fields. At the end of each working day, the farmer would "reach into his pocket and divide the change among us," recalls George. Sometimes they worked all day for a grand total of 80 cents apiece.

But, as Mary Poppins sang, "in every job that must be done, there is an element of fun." They managed to turn some of their work into a game. Semi-rotten tomatoes flew across the field in impromptu food fights. Skinny kids like George got revenge on neighborhood bullies by lobbing "cow pies" at them from safe distances. Once, George Jr. threw one of these at a big mean fellow and hit him square in the head. "I tell you," he laughs, "I ran for probably two miles! He never caught me. If he would have, I wouldn't be here today!"

Mabel's brother wanted the Parmer kids to work at his farm. He offered young George Jr. free room and board, an opportunity usually eagerly accepted by most depression-era families. But Mabel said no. She knew that her brother drastically overworked children, from sunup to sunset, sometimes putting them on dangerous equipment or giving them tasks way beyond their abilities. "She probably saved my life!" says George.

Delores cleaned houses on Saturdays for $1.00 per day. "I thought I was rich!" she laughs. Ten-year-old Jean went to live with a sick neighbor during the summer. She cleaned house, pulled weeds, milked cows, collected eggs, and babysat for $2.50 a week, plus room and board. Both girls bought much-needed school clothes with the earnings.

On weekend evenings, George Sr. and Jr. often drove to the Dalmatia firehouse to watch boxing matches on the firefighters' television. When electricity finally came to their area and they acquired a radio, George Jr. also signed boxing matches for his father, blow-by-blow. His hands flew through left jabs, right hooks, uppercuts and knockdowns. It brings new meaning to the expression "knock yourself out," doesn't it?

From time to time, the two Georges traveled to Philadelphia to attend A's games. They especially liked Sunday double-headers. George says, "Many times we'd see [the A's] play the Yankees and [they'd] lose the first game." But, ever optimistic, the two Georges would stay through the end of the second game. "The Yankees [would be leading] 7 to 1 in the ninth inning, but we would stay, hoping for a rally which never seemed to come."

He and his dad saw some of baseball's greatest players at those games: Mickey Mantle, Roger Maris, Phil "The Scooter" Ruzzoto, Allie Reynolds, Ferris Fain, Carl Scheib, Bobby Shantz, and Ted Williams – to name just a few. When the A's moved to Kansas City and then Oakland, the Phillies became his dad's "second best team." They attended some of those games too, watching players Stan Musial, Steve Carlton, and Jim Konstanty.

But the A's are still near and dear to George Jr.'s heart. Now in his 70s, he is still an A's fan and "always will be," he admits.[8]

Young George developed a reputation as a practical joker and a bit of a daredevil. He consumed weird food combinations to gross out his sisters. One afternoon, he snuck up behind his mother and clamped his hand over her mouth. Alarmed and frightened, she scratched him deeply all the way down his forearm. She was horrified she had hurt him, but he was appropriately contrite. He never did that again.

All three siblings attended Lower Mahanoy School, a one-room building housing twelve grades. On their daily bus rides, George mortified his sisters by singing popular songs at the top of his lungs, to the encouragement and delight of the other students.

Despite their precarious economic situation, the Parmers took in Mabel's niece and nephew. Young George made a running gag out of making his mother think that his cousin Bill was kicking him under the dinner table. Mabel would angrily "chew Bill out" and even though her speech was somewhat difficult to understand, there was no mistaking her ire. "But Bill hadn't done anything!" laughs Delores.

One frosty winter day when he was 12 or 13 years old, George Jr. became suddenly and poignantly aware of how poor his family was. He was sliding around on the ice on the Mahantango Creek by his home. Not on skates, mind you –

---

8   George is also an avid Penn State fan. He probably holds the record for the greatest collection of PSU merchandise and paraphernalia outside of the university itself!

his family couldn't afford such a luxury. Instead, he made do as best he could, running and sliding across the frozen surface in his boots. Suddenly, he lost his balance and flipped backward. His head banged hard on the ice and he ended up flat on his back, dazed and hurting. He laid there quietly on the ice for a few minutes, hot tears slipping down his cold cheeks, and a wave of deep sadness washed over him. His family was really and truly poor. The realization affected him deeply and he remembers praying, "Lord, will you help me get ahead?" He admits now that he doesn't know if that was a good prayer or not – he wasn't a Christian at the time – but it was honest, humble, and heartfelt.

He was also aware that what his family did possess was an abundance of love and emotional security, the kind of things money can't buy. George and Mabel's deafness formed an unbreakable family bond. Through their children, they interacted more effectively with the hearing world. "We were our parents' ears," explains Jean. As a result, the Parmer children developed a strong and early sense of responsibility, confidence, and deep compassion for others.

Jean accompanied her father when he finally landed an important interview for a long-term janitorial position at the Pennsylvania Department of Highways. When the interviewing director expressed doubts about hiring him, Jean pleaded, "Won't you please give my Daddy a job?" Her appeal touched the interviewer's heart and George Sr. got the position. He worked there for the rest of his life.

Meanwhile, Mabel worked as a hand seamstress at the Dalmatia Shirt Factory. Rising at 5:30 a.m. every morning, she walked four or five miles to work and then repeated the trip each evening, a walk that took an hour each way.

George Sr. drove an old Willys[9] automobile to Harrisburg every day. The vehicle was fine for the commute, provided George wasn't in a hurry. Its motor was a bit sluggish and it struggled on the hilly back roads of northern Dauphin county. On family outings, the children often had to get out and push it up the hills. Delores laughs, "A dog could run faster than that car!" She wasn't kidding. One time a stray dog raced the car uphill and was long gone while the Willys stalled and slowly rolled back down again.

As the children grew into teenagers, George and Mabel kept a close eye on them. The kids' evenings around the juke box at the local Prest Troutman's soda bar had to end early for them. They knew that Mabel would be waiting at the front window and they didn't want her stay up late after a long week at work. She always greeted them in the drive-way with a lantern, no matter what time it was. And she never gave her girls too much time to enjoy too many stolen good-night kisses!

By the mid-1950s, both Delores and Jean were married and living on their own. George Sr., Mabel, and George Jr. moved to Harrisburg, closer to George Sr.'s employment. They settled in Hooverter Homes, a low-income housing development, also known as "The Projects."

It was a bit of a rough neighborhood. Young George Jr. was teased for his "Dutchified" accent when he entered tenth grade at John Harris High School. His sisters worried about what the future would hold for him. College was out of the question. The family had no money for that. He would

---

9   One model of the Willys automobile became today's Jeep.

have to find a job somewhere, somehow, to provide enough income to support a family someday. What in the world could he do?

George[10] wondered too. He was strong and big, so he signed on as a laborer for a cross-country moving company during summer breaks. The company's owner was a street-smart ex-con who, George asserts, "always looked out for me and taught me a lot." Traveling across the country gave George a deeper understanding of American culture, an edge, he says, that would later prove helpful in life.

He stayed with the moving company for about six months after graduation. Although it had been interesting, a life on the road was not what he wanted. He married his girlfriend Betty and landed a job with Harrisburg Grocery, a whole-sale food distributor. His first job was tax-stamping packs of cigarettes at a starting wage of $1.00 per hour.

The company's owners were excellent businessmen and taught George the fundamentals of accounting and cus-tomer service. His big break came when one of the sales people was caught embezzling funds. George was promoted into that position and received a salary plus commissions. It was 1960 and he was 21 years old.

His sales territory covered a large section of central and eastern Pennsylvania, from Lewistown to York to Allen-town. He often rose at 5 or 6 AM and was on the road until 10 PM. He enjoyed his work and stayed at Harrisburg Gro-cery for eight years. Eventually, he controlled the top sales territory and earned about $14,000 per year, a nice salary in the 1960s. He actually made more money than the sales

---

10   From this point on, George Jr. will be referred to simply as "George."

manager at the time, which caused some resentment from both his co-workers and his boss.

His boss's management style left a lot to be desired. He browbeat his salespeople, a practice that George decided he was never going to do if he was ever in a leadership role. When George was in Texas for National Guard training, his boss took his wife Betty shopping to make sure she had everything she needed while George was away. George appreciated that, but afterwords he noticed that this kindness had a sharp edge to it. While taking care of Betty, he also quietly cut George's pay. When George found out, he was understandably angry and the practice of "cutting someone's pay" was added to the list of things he would never do if he ever became a boss.

That incident also convinced him that it was time to move on, so he started looking around for self-employment business opportunities. He had always been good at numbers, so he found an accounting franchise that he thought he could try. The franchise cost $4900. He didn't have that much money saved, so he decided to take on a partner. The sales manager at Harrisburg Grocery liked the idea also, so they pooled their resources to buy the franchise.

And they sharpened their #2 lead pencils.

CHAPTER TWO

I n the first year of the accounting business, George made a whopping $700. The next year his income increased to $3000. It was the late '60s, early '70s. No computers, no fancy accounting software, no internet. Just adding machines and pencils, spreadsheets and tax code books. George obtained his license as a Pennsylvania Public Accountant and rolled up his sleeves.

It's an understatement to say times were tough. He readily admits that would not have made it during those years if Betty hadn't been working full time to keep them going.

Further deepening his struggle, his beloved mother Mabel passed away. It was a quiet passing. One morning she and George Sr. woke; she made breakfast and wrote up a grocery list for him to take to the store. When he returned from shopping, he found her lying on their bed as if asleep. But when he checked her, he realized she was dead. Her cause of death was never determined. She was only 68 years old.

George pressed on. His was not a job for the fainthearted. At its peak, his franchise had over ten employees and served approximately 175 business clients and over 700 individual tax clients. From January through April 14th, George worked 14-hour days, seven days a week. He always approached the tax season with enthusiasm, but by the end of it he "couldn't stop shaking" from the anxiety and pressure. To top it off, the main office of the franchise got it-self into financial trouble and went out of business, putting George in a real pickle.

Without the support and expertise of the now-defunct franchise, George spent countless after-office hours se-questered in his house, studying the ever-changing tax laws to fulfill his clients' needs. Many of his customers were small business owners who desperately needed sound tax advice and George enjoyed educating them about how to handle their money. He cautioned them against practic-es that could bring trouble from the IRS and they appreciat-ed his wisdom and integrity. Helping others succeed would become one of the guiding principles of his business philos-ophy.[11]

But the pace was grueling and eventually George was ready to move on. At the same time, one of his builder cli-ents had been victimized by an embezzler so George decid-ed to try to help him. He researched modular home building franchises, which sounded to him like an "up and coming thing." Then he approached another client, a local maga-zine publisher, and asked him if he'd be interested in part-nering with him to purchase a modular home franchise. His client liked the idea and agreed. They incorporated Fine Line Homes (FLH) in February of 1972.

George admits that he would not have gotten into home building if it hadn't been for his desire to help his builder friend. That friend helped him get the business going and after he left, George became more involved. But, he admits,

---

11   To this day, he regularly encounters former clients who thank him for his guidance during his early years as a tax consultant.

he was still quite a novice. "I knew absolutely nothing about the building business," he laughs. This was made abundantly clear one day when their newly-hired sales rep came to him and his partner with a question. A customer wanted soffits over his kitchen cabinets. "What do you think that will cost?" she asked them. They looked at each other blankly. She shook her head. "You guys don't know what soffits are, do you?" They were totally clueless.

But in time George learned the ropes. Eventually he bought out his partner and became sole owner of FLH. But the company struggled to survive in a difficult market and before long it racked up $50,000 of debt. "We owed everybody," George recalls. In a desperate effort to save the company, he visited every creditor with a plan. He promised to purchase all of his supplies from that point on with cash and each time, he would add extra funds to be put toward FLH's outstanding debt. "I think I can have you paid off in a year and a half or two years," he told them. Amazingly, every one of his creditors agreed to that plan. George followed through and satisfied all the overdue accounts within the promised time.

He was soon able to increase his staff so he hired a real estate broker and an administrative assistant. Dolores Katz became his "right hand woman." She was a no-nonsense lady, unafraid to speak her mind and tell George bluntly, if necessary, "I think you're wrong." She became vice-president of Fine Line during an era when it was unheard of to have a woman in a position of authority in a corporate setting, let alone a construction company. To George, that didn't matter one little bit. If someone could handle responsibility and wasn't afraid to make decisions, he gave him – or her – authority within his organization. More importantly, he listened to their advice, supported their ideas, and encouraged them to succeed.

In the early years, the company was desperate for work. They handled scattered-lot building all over central Pennsylvania, Maryland, and Virginia. "There were many, many Fridays when payroll was due and I didn't have the money," George remembers. He often tapped into his private funds to cover expenses.

One of the difficulties within the modular home industry in the 1970s was how it was perceived by the public. Many people equated them with mobile homes and thought they were inferior to stick-built homes. But the truth is that modular builders must follow standard residential building codes and their homes are built as solidly as any other.

But the public was difficult to convince. One time when George and his crew unloaded one of their homes onto its foundation in an established neighborhood, residents suddenly emerged from their houses and began screaming at him. They strongly objected to the fact that it was a modular. Even the building inspector, who issued the permit, was angry. But George stayed calm and steady and the house placement proceeded as planned. When it was finished, it looked like every other house in the development and fit in perfectly. The furor quickly died down. George had proven his point.

Meeting payroll tax obligations was another hurdle that FLH found difficult to overcome in the early days. The company fell into delinquency at one point, prompting a visit from the IRS. But George assured the agents that all he needed was a little extra time to catch up. Amazingly, the IRS gave it to him. He was true to his word. When he made the final payment that brought the taxes up-to-date, he was never delinquent on his taxes again. "Ever," he emphasizes.

He credits his survival during those lean years to his employees, suppliers, and his banker. "You realize that you can't make it totally by yourself. You need a lot of people to help you. I [acquired] a basic core of people who were dedicated and willing to learn." Fulton Bank stood by him through the lean years too. "It's still my bank today," George affirms.

In 1977, George realized he could take advantage of a unique tax break to improve FLH's bottom line and help him track construction costs. He decided to pay his employees through a separate company. He called this new entity the Pay Company, which was shortened to Payco. In essence, Payco would employ the staff for FLH. Each FLH employee who transferred over to Payco qualified for a tax credit for the company. It was an accounting coup that gave George a much-needed financial boost.

By the late '70s, mortgage interest rates had risen through the proverbial roof – up to 17% or more in some areas of the state. Most buyers simply could not afford to finance a home at those rates. To improve sales, George found a way to offer low-interest VA housing loans for purchasers of Fine Line homes and also pursued financing for his customers through the VA.

The downside was that both programs required time-consuming paperwork that clogged up his cash flow. One afternoon, when the company was particularly desperate for funds, George drove to the VA office in Philadelphia to collect the final documents that he needed to expedite a settlement. When he arrived, the VA staff informed him that the paperwork wouldn't be ready for several days.

"Well, I'm going to have to wait," he told them.

"But they won't be ready for days," they said.

"Well, I'll wait," he repeated, and promptly made himself comfortable in the waiting area. "People came out and looked at me as if I were some kind of maniac," he laughs. "But I was not leaving."

Three hours later, he had the documents.

George thinks the turning point for FLH was when he purchased ground for its first 10-lot development in 1978. It wasn't a smooth sail though. His initial euphoria quickly turned into deep concern. When he arrived at the township office to obtain development permits, he was informed that if the property was within 1000 feet of the public water main he would be required to install water lines to every home. That would mean tunneling under a busy two-lane road, an expensive operation for his little building company.

"I'm dead in the water," he thought. His engineer immediately drove over to the property and started measuring. George remembers, "The distance was 1005 feet. Five feet over a thousand!" Fine Line could drill wells and avoid the high expense of installing public water lines. "Those five feet saved the company," he says.

The lots in that development, priced at about $12,000

each, sold out within 90 days. With the proceeds, George established a profit-sharing bonus program for his employees. But that wasn't all. Realizing that many of them had no financial plans for their retirement, he asked them if they'd like him to put additional funds into IRAs. All 30 employees told him they preferred immediate cash. "I was just flabbergasted," George recalls. He boldly overrode their decision and established the retirement accounts anyway. "There was some grumbling," he admits, but years later many of them thanked George for his foresight. In fact, one long-time employee confessed to George that if had he been given that cash as a young man he would have "drunk it up." Those IRAs grew and are now distributing much-appreciated funds to retirees.

During the 1970s, Congress tightened regulations on the building industry in response to an increase in consumer housing complaints. The National Association of Home Builders (NAHB) established a ten-year warranty organization named the Home Owners' Warranty Company (HOW). Through HOW, homeowners could obtain insurance to cover possible structural defects in their homes.

By that time, FLH had discontinued placing modular homes. It now assembled "panelized" homes, using Ryan Building Systems based in McKeesport, PA. Cost-effective and well-designed, these houses were shipped in kits to building sites and assembled according to detailed instructions. George was confident about Ryan's high-quality construction standards, so FLH became an early charter member of HOW and began offering home warranties to Fine Line homeowners.

However, a storm was brewing. In1980, HOW raised its rates retroactively. At the time, FLH had contracts for over 75 new homes, with warranties priced at the old rates. George asked HOW if the warranties on those homes could be grandfathered in at the cost in effect at the time their sales contracts had been signed. HOW refused and insisted that Fine Line had to pay the new higher rates. George felt that HOW had thrown down the gauntlet and that it needed some competition. Consequently, in February 1981, he and a partner established Residential Warranty Corporation (RWC).

Unfortunately, the partnership soon unraveled. "Partners are great," George muses, "but to be frank, they don't always have the same agenda." His partner was happy with the status quo and seemed reluctant to push the business to the next level. In addition, although the partner had not invested anything toward the original RWC start-up costs, he pressed George for a 50-50 split of the profit. George was already generously paying him 40% to run it because his partner needed a job when they started RWC. But George didn't think an increase was fair or warranted.

The breakup of the partnership was acrimonious and finally went into litigation. The two owners came to an agreement, literally "on the courthouse steps." RWC employees waited nervously back at the office during the dramatic resolution, calling it the company's "Waterloo." George returned that day as the sole owner of RWC. One long-time employee confirms, "Having George...[become] the president of RWC was the best thing that ever happened to this company."

It was a swift transition. "All of a sudden," says George, "I'm running a warranty company. RWC was in Camp Hill, Fine line was on Eisenhower Boulevard [in Harrisburg]." That arrangement was inefficient. "So, I bought a place down in Highspire…and brought RWC and Fine line into the same building," he recalls, adding with a chuckle, "and I sat in the middle."

The first floor of the Highspire building was occupied by a White Shield pharmacy and Scooperman, a restaurant/ice-cream parlor, owned by one of his former business associates. George thought he would probably need that space eventually, so he purchased Scooperman also. His employees thoroughly enjoyed the unique benefit of going downstairs for ice cream, donuts, and sandwiches any time they wanted. But, he laughs, "it didn't take long to realize that I made a horrendous mistake being in the ice cream business!" He finally closed the store after a particularly disastrous episode involving an employee, an open freezer door, and gallons of rapidly melting ice cream. For years afterward, George was criticized by local residents for his decision to close Scooperman. He laughs, "I'd be pumping gas and someone would say, 'Your name Parmer? You the guy who shut down the ice cream shop? Why did you do that?'"

Long-time employees remember dozens of stories recounting the shenanigans and escapades that characterized those early days in Highspire. Employees took turns cleaning toilets, endured traveling mishaps and good-natured practical jokes, and removed dead varmints from the attic. Some ventured out onto the makeshift deck over the pharmacy and occasionally one would step on a weak area of the roof and his or her foot would poke through the ceiling into the retail space below. Needless to say, this startled pharmacy employees and customers alike. Eventually the White Shield owner called to chastise George for not honoring the "peace and tranquility" clause of the lease. (George readily agreed and patched the roof.) These stories and more have become legends in the Parmer corporate family.[12]

Sue Kent, George's personal administrative assistant, reminisces, "I have to admit…although we're more prosperous today, I liked the early days because I got to do everything. Everybody knew everybody. We were really tightly knit. It was great."

An opportunity for the expansion of Fine Line Homes came in the early '80s. George's sister Jean's husband passed away and his business, Harris Homes (HH) in northern Pennsylvania, wasn't doing very well. She and her sons approached George to take a look at its operations and give them some advice. He visited their office and what he saw shocked him. Jean and her sons gave George the power to make any changes he thought would be necessary, so he immediately set to work cutting expenses and reducing the number of employees. However, those measures proved insufficient to improve HH's bottom line.

But George had an idea. If he purchased Harris Homes and merged its $1.5 million net operating loss with Fine Line's profit, he would be able to reduce FLH's tax liability until the HH loss was eliminated. It would be a win-win situation for both businesses. In 1985, he bought Harris Homes and its associated land development entity, Eastern

---

12   For details, see *It All Began with a Number Two Lead Pencil*, Company Edition, 2004, Morris Publishing, Kearney, NE.

Development and Planning.

The first thing he did was raise home prices $5000 across-the-board to improve HH's operating margin. He brought the HH management staff to Harrisburg for training and insisted that they review their accounting books regularly and take responsibility for the company's future profitability.

In deference to the company's autonomy, George declined to change the Harris Homes name to Fine Line Homes. But after a year or two, when Harris Homes finally recovered, its management team came to George requesting to be part of Fine Line. George explains, "By not being aggressive [about changing their name right away], by letting them come to us, they were behind the idea. I think that was critical."

George discontinued building panelized Ryan homes and began building from original blueprints. Job versatility was again the name of the game. All construction employees received on-the-job training in every phase of the building process. Plumbers learned how to hang siding, roofers learned how to paint, trim carpenters learned how to install flooring. "It wasn't boring!" one employee laughs.

They made a lot of mistakes along the way. Deliveries were inefficient. Storage was difficult to access. Job site conditions were often uncomfortable, if not borderline dangerous. "We were so stupid way back then," one employee remembers, with a laugh. "George just turned us loose and we tried. Everything I've learned [since] I've been here has been by making mistakes. We just worked and worked and worked until we got it perfect."

Employees carried materials to and from the job site in

their personal automobiles. The electrician's lime green '73 Plymouth sagged so much from the extra weight of tools and supplies that he had to have "helper springs" installed on his rear shock absorbers. George acquired an old rusty '50s model stake body truck with a wooden bed and they stuffed it with as many building supplies as they could. One employee thought that truck needed a paint job, so he took it home one afternoon and covered it with blue spray paint. He thought it looked great until he saw it the next morning. An overnight rain shower had turned the solid blue truck into a polka-dotted wonder. Despite the unique paint job, its days were numbered. Eventually it died a dramatic death when its engine blew up, belching dark smoke across the PA turnpike.

FLH employees went back to hauling materials in their own cars again, but not for long. George finally scraped together several hundred dollars and bought a used Bell Telephone vehicle at a local auction. As funds became available, more of the distinctive army green vans were added to fledgling FLH truck fleet

By 1984, Fine Line was building over 100 homes per year. The company had doubled, perhaps tripled, its business in a few short years. By the late '80s, the Harrisburg operation had fully transitioned from scattered lot building to community home sales.

One fateful afternoon, George had an epiphany. He realized that he could buy many common building supplies directly from manufacturers if he purchased them in bulk through an intermediary entity. And fortunately, he already had an entity waiting in the wings to take on this new role – little "Pay Company" Payco. He changed its name to Payco Building Supply (PBS) and began purchasing large quantities of the most frequently used Fine Line building materials. Payco sold those items to FLH at below retail prices, saving money for Fine Line while also making money for Payco.

But the transition was not as easy as it sounds. As a payroll and staffing company, Payco had required no more than a good accounting program and a few office personnel. Now it needed a place to store bulky supplies and knowledgeable employees to handle them.

Initially, they stored things in scattered locations such as the basements of model homes, in a barn on George's personal property, and throughout Harrisburg in rented garages. Items accumulated into inaccessible stacks. Employees spent a lot of valuable time traveling from makeshift warehouse to makeshift warehouse, moving inventory from one stack to another. The inefficiency quickly began eroding the company's bottom line.

George knew that he would need a larger, centrally-located facility if PBS was going to be profitable. He finally found a warehouse on Fulling Mill Road in Middletown and moved all the inventory there. Soon, that building was bulging at the seams, so he rented an adjacent warehouse, effectively doubling the space. PBS has continued to expand since, now occupying a building of over 60,000 square feet and still growing.

George learned few lessons the hard way as PBS expanded its product line. One misstep involved a simple well-known faucet and George's love for baseball. "This product was presented to me by an ex-professional baseball player who played on one of my favorite teams," he recalls. The decision to purchase that line had nothing to do with the price or the quality of the product.

PBS bought dozens of the faucets and began installing them. It wasn't long before George realized he'd made a mistake. The faucets left a lot to be desired. "To make a long story short, we had to go back and replace every one of them," he laments. He never made a product choice based on a celebrity endorsement ever again.

Meanwhile, the demand for home warranties was growing and RWC grew along with it. Home warranty coverage is not an insurance policy, but it must be backed by a legal insurer. This caused some tricky transitions.

In the beginning, RWC insured its warranties through Illinois Employers of Wausau. That insurer and several others eventually either folded or backed out of warranty coverage, putting RWC in a tough spot.

United Equitable in Chicago, originally a car warranty company, approached George and invited him to tour their offices and discuss becoming RWC's insurer. In August of 1988 he flew to Chicago and met UE's owner. At the end of the tour George "got all the way to the back of the building and saw two printers, spitting out checks faster than you can count." The checks were for the previous day's claims. George knew that United Equitable couldn't survive for long if it was paying that number of claims on a daily basis. UE's owner admitted that he needed George's business to generate additional revenue. But since George needed a large nationwide insurer, he gave UE his business and, for the time being, RWC was safe.

But George knew UE would not go on for long. He had already started his own Eastern Atlantic Insurance Company in 1986 to cover his own warranty business, but its coverage territory was limited. Because of this and his concerns about United Equitable, George began gathering information about establishing a risk retention group (RRG), a larger insurance company that can provide nationwide coverage. At that time, RWC couldn't generate the volume of business to support this venture. But in 1988 George acquired Builders Trust Warranty, a Florida firm, and paired its business with RWC with the hope of eventually achieving the volume that would be necessary for the RRG.

By that time RWC had become one of the largest home warranty companies in the nation. The insurance commission eventually realized that United Equitable was in trouble and put it into rehabilitation, meaning that it could no longer underwrite any new business from RWC. But George's foresight paid off and his RRG was approved for business within two weeks of the shutdown of United Equitable. "A lot of people thought I was taking a big risk [starting an RRG], and I probably was," George recalls. "But sometimes you have to do those kinds of things."

George moved ahead to establish an additional insurance entity: Western Pacific Mutual Insurance Corporation (WPMIC). It is domiciled in Colorado and when George approached the state to establish it he was told that he would be required to have $250,000 in cash and a $500,000 letter of credit from a national bank to qualify. No problem, he thought, and called Fulton Bank. However, Fulton Bank is not a national bank. Uh, oh, he thought. Not to worry, they told him. We have a national bank in our network. It was Swineford National Bank in northern Pennsylvania. "Swineford!" George laughs. Western Pacific was funded by a PIGGY bank!

WPMIC enabled RWC to expand its business into all 50 states and is reinsured through Lloyds of London. Since 2001, WPMIC has consistently received excellent A- ratings from A.M. Best, the agency that evaluates insurance companies, and now controls an equity surplus of over $100 million.

George's affinity for modular homes prompted him to offer warranties to modular home owners also. In 1989 he established Manufactured Housing Warranty Corporation (MHWC), a separate entity under the RWC umbrella.

Unfortunately, during this time, his marriage struggled and eventually he and Betty divorced. "That was a traumatic time," George admits, "extremely stressful and painful." Shortly afterward he and his second wife Barbara were married. Their son Adam was born in early 1991, followed the next year by daughter Eve.

Now he had a busy family to go with his rapidly growing business. For him, it was that "sandwich" season of life, active little children at home and a slowly deteriorating aging parent who needed greater supervision. His father George was now in his 80s, still lived on his own and still drove his car. But after a series of fender benders – one involving a young mother and child – George realized that he would have to commit the dreaded "tough love" act of taking away his dad's car keys. "That was really, really hard," George admits. He and Barbara picked him up regularly for shopping and doctor visits. His father continued to live alone for a short time after that, but eventually he needed skilled nursing care. He passed away in 1994.

By this time RWC's staff had grown to occupy the entire Highspire building, so FLH moved to its current location on Derry Street in Harrisburg. Then RWC eventually outgrew the Highspire office, so George renovated an old Weis Market west of the FLH office for RWC's new headquarters. Both businesses have Derry street addresses: Fine Line at 7300, RWC at 5300 - easy to remember!

RWC didn't know it at the time, but all that new spacious office space would soon be a hive of frantic activity. By 1994, HOW's books, available to the public, increasingly resembled "smoke and mirrors," George recalls. By the end of that year, the insurance department forced it to fold, leaving builders high and dry without adequate warranty protection.

RWC braced itself for the avalanche of business coming its way. Sure enough, phones began ringing off the hook and business doubled overnight. His staff worked 12-14 hour days, going above and beyond the call of duty to make sure builders had coverage. "It was the wildest time this company ever had!" George recalls. "It illustrated to me the importance of having a seasoned staff whose performance and experience can meet the extra demands."

Checks from panicked builders flooded into RWC's accounts. RWC required builders to send certified checks for between $100,000 to $200,000 to secure their warranties until background checks could be done to affirm their business' financial viability. Mailbags full of these payments arrived daily at the RWC office and keeping track of the checks became a daunting task. In fact, at one point, a $100,000 check went missing, prompting a frantic search that ended up with one intrepid employee being lowered into the dumpster to sift through the day's trash. (Alas, the check never did turn up.)

With this sudden influx of funds, George Aldus Parmer found himself surfing a huge financial wave. Now he had to stay on the board.

CHAPTER THREE

I n the early 1990s, RWC expanded into Texas, a warranty market with unique challenges. Some parts of the state are plagued by "active soils" that expand and contract as weather conditions fluctuate between drought and flooding. Building foundations in these areas are in constant danger of shifting and cracking, producing damage that can cause an entire structure to weaken and fail.

When George purchased Home Owner's Multiple Equity (HOME) of Texas, he kept the entity separate from RWC because if this increased risk. Senior Vice President Kathy Foley says there are more claims in Texas than any other part of the country. To minimize this risk, HOME does not offer home warranties in the areas of Texas where active soils are a major problem. This conservative approach has kept HOME of Texas viable in a state that other warranty companies have abandoned.

Not every Parmer business venture has been a home run. One company that "went up in smoke," as George says, is Residential Technology Systems (RTS). This entity was established in 1996 to provide structured wiring in new homes for new technologies. In retrospect, he says, it was ahead of its time. "People weren't ready for it and it couldn't get traction." It also didn't help that technologies were changing so quickly that by the time wiring was installed, it was already obsolete. Although George folded RTS as a separate entity, Fine Line Homes still provides up-to-date technological connectivity in its homes.

Another defunct company is IntegraTech, established in 1997. Its purpose was to provide third-party builder call-back services for new homeowners. It started off strong, but died during the contraction of the building industry in 2007.

RWC's Insurance Advantage program, on the other hand, has done extremely well. Initiated in 1998, it covers the gap between the builder's warranty and general liability coverage.

George is a "do it ourselves" kind of guy and always prefers to have most services provided by his own staff. In January 1999, George purchased George E. Zimmerman Real Estate. It became Fine Line Realty, the in-house brokerage for Fine Line Homes.

In July of 2000, George repurposed the land development company he had acquired in the Harris Homes deal. It was rebranded as Eastern Communities and purchases property for all Fine Line developments. By this time FLH had expanded into four locations beyond the Harrisburg market: Lewisburg, Hazleton, Sayre, and State College.

Meanwhile, Eastern Atlantic Insurance wasn't doing as well as George liked. It had been outsourcing all of its reinsurance needs and only held a few million dollars in capital. George decided to discontinue using reinsurers and called all the Eastern Atlantic staff together. From that point on, he told them, they were going to handle it themselves.

He established Integrity Underwriters/Administrators to provide internal claims management services for Eastern Atlantic. As a result, Eastern Atlantic's revenue soared. By 2008 it received its first A- rating from A.M. Best, which it has maintained every year since. It now handles $18-20 million annual premium with over $30 million in capital and surplus to cover claims. Bringing everything "in-house" made all the difference.

Fine Line Homes, Residential Warranty Company, and Payco are separate companies financially and legally, but exist in a symbiotic economic relationship. Insurance companies like RWC collect cash up front and manage it according to strict legal guidelines. Building companies like FLH collect cash in deposits and draws. Supply companies like Payco behave like retail stores. All the companies support and interact with each other. Financial "firewalls" are in place to prevent a major blow to one company from affecting the others.

Business hummed along through the early 2000s. Says RWC's VP Kathy Foley, "From 2002 to 2007 the real estate market hit its peak. Business was coming to us; we didn't have to go find it. Everybody was happy."

But the economic recession that started in 2007 took the wind out of everyone's sails. "The bottom fell out hard," Kathy Foley remembers. "Every aspect of the building industry tanked. More builders declared bankruptcy in those years than any other time in our nation's history. Companies that had been in business for 30 or 40 years went belly-up. Not only did the companies fail, but business owners lost much of their personal wealth as well."

The following chart demonstrates the rapid demise of many U.S. building firms:

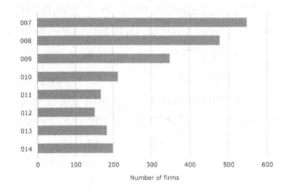

Source:http://www.softwareadvice.com/construction/industryview/ecosystem-reces-sion-vs-2014/

All of the Parmer companies are associated with the building industry, so they all contracted. RWC experienced only one uptick and unfortunately it was in an undesirable parameter: the number of claims. Because a warranty "steps into the shoes of the builder," Mrs. Foley explains, RWC had to cover claims it ordinarily wouldn't have had to handle because some of its builders went belly-up. "It was like a bloodbath for a while."

Despite the downturn, RWC did not raise rates or alter its products. Mrs. Foley reports that although their member mega-builders were only doing half of the amount of building they had done previously, that amount was sufficient to carry RWC.

Fine Line Homes, along with most other mid-Atlantic builders, experienced a sharp decrease in construction starts. John Kerschner, Senior VP of FLH, admits that Fine Line, like other major builders, found itself with a large inventory of unsold homes. They weren't "bad" houses, but were left over during the downturn and became somewhat obsolete. "We needed a 'cash for clunkers' program for homes," he laughs. He eventually sold many of them through innovative two-year "rent-to-own" programs and three-year "zero-percent-purchase" programs.

Fine Line also initiated a Mortgage Payment Protection Plan for buyers who had concerns about the economy and their job security. This program covered six mortgage payments if a FLH homebuyer lost his or her job within the first two years after purchase. That safety net eased the minds of reluctant buyers and also helped Fine Line move inventory.

To appeal to a new buyer demographic, the FLH staff proactively used the slowdown to fine tune its fine lines. They carefully reviewed all their building plans. Some were retained, others were modified, and still others were scrapped. The old model homes were moved and repurposed, or – in the case of the Sayre/Milan office – torn down.

Designers drafted brand-new floor plans to take advantage of emerging trends in the building industry. Homes now included larger outdoor living spaces (patios, porches, and three-season rooms), luxury high-end kitchen appliances and finishes, and universal access features for an aging population (wider hallways, fewer stairs, and elevator options). For young families, plans included larger laundry rooms, security systems, nanny-cams, and improved storage options. All homes were upgraded to be more energy-efficient and environmentally-friendly.

Before the downturn, FLH had restricted the number and

kind of modifications homeowners could make to their chosen plan. But increased competition and broader consumer choices in the marketplace made George realize that Fine Line needed to be more flexible. Although it's not a custom home builder, FLH now allows home buyers a wide variety of personalized changes to any basic floor plan.

In the middle of the crash, unused and obsolete inventory piled up at Payco's warehouse. George sold some of these items at auction in Lancaster, PA, but only realized a return of ten cents on the dollar. Not satisfied with that, he began researching other sales outlets. He hired a savvy IT fellow from Boston – Jim Richardson – to help him market the items online.

Jim began offering inventory on sites such as eBay and Overstock.com and – lo and behold! – achieved a dollar for dollar return. This successful foray into online marketing morphed into two new entities: Your Home Supply (YHS) and InterShip. By 2013, YHS had emerged from a field of over 700 companies in the Overstock network to become its #1 partner, based on timely delivery, fewest short ships, returns and reviews. YHS became the Parmer company rainbow during the perfect-storm recession.

George admits that he had "never seen [a downturn] quite like this" in his lifetime. Extreme layoffs, which George hated, kept the company viable. Those were hard business decisions, Kathy Foley muses. The RWC sales force had to be reduced by 50% - all good people, George says sadly.

To boost the spirits of his remaining staff and member builders, he wrote encouraging upbeat editorials in the Residential Recap and The Scoop, the company newsletters. His articles addressed subjects relevant to both groups such as fighting the urge to use lower quality items, financial planning for builders, insurer reliability, supervising subcontractors, controlling proliferation of added building costs, warning about future corrections to housing/real estate markets, making long-term plans to invest in your business, watching costs, home financing, reputation in the market, addressing the downturn (safeguards and discipline), and land development reform.

Negative rumors occasionally circulated about the health and viability of the Parmer companies. He dispelled those by publishing summaries of each company's financial strength to reassure staff that the companies would survive. He also reminded them that RWC was the only national warranty program that remained under its original stable leadership. With careful forethought and planning, this captain would use every ounce of his keen business sense to keep the ship afloat.

George fueled the online sales of YHS by expanding the inventory with new cabinet hardware that could be easily stored and shipped. These items sold like hotcakes. Encouraged, he sought a manufacturer to develop a unique YHS line of hardware, christened Stonemill Hardware. An overseas company won the contract and Stonemill Hardware became its own entity in 2010. It currently brings in revenue of approximately $25,000/week. In addition, YHS obtained the rights to use official collegiate branding for a new specialty line of hardware, featuring major U.S. university logos. It is the only company that manufactures and distributes such a product.

Meanwhile, the single-family home industry had been hit especially hard. In the Fall, 2011, issue of the Residential Recap, George noted, "The census bureau has put housing starts at an all-time low since 1959 when they began keeping records." The recession "officially" ended in 2009, but economic recovery has been sluggish.

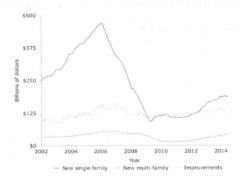

Source: U.S. Census, Construction Spending, July 2014 (http://www.census.gov/construction/c30/c30index.html)

During the crash, one particular trend caught George's eye. "Smaller, niche construction firms have been able to carve out their place in the economic playground. While fewer homes are being built, many people are opting to renovate and improve their homes—increasing their homes' value, while also driving business to these niche firms."[13]

The Residential Recap issue of Fall 2016, highlights this new niche market:

"Remodelers reported that the following projects were

---

13   http://www.softwareadvice.com/construction/industryview/ecosystem-recession-vs-2014/

more common than in 2013:

- Whole house remodels increased by 10%
- Room additions increased by 12%
- Finished basements increased by 8%
- Bathroom additions increased by 7%

Bathrooms topped the list of most common remodeling projects for the fifth time since 2010. 81% of remodelers reported that bathrooms were a common remodeling job for their company while 79% percent of remodelers reported the same for kitchen remodels. Window and door replacements decreased to 36% from 45% in 2014." (Original source for statistics: NAHB)

To take advantage of this possible new revenue stream, George established Harrisburg Kitchen and Bath (HKB), a residential remodeling firm. He tapped his new son-in-law, Keith Dolon, to head it. Keith had some experience with construction and product installation and a degree in IT and Business from Messiah College. But he admits that formal coursework doesn't fully prepare students for the real business world. He had a lot to learn, including a few basics, when he joined the Parmer Companies. Fortunately he's a quick learner.

Keith has the same steady work ethic of his father-in-law. In addition to his current job as Vice President and Manager of Payco, he also manages Stonemill Hardware, HKB, and InterShip, and several other entities. Keith does whatever needs to be done to keep things going. That sometimes includes the nitty-gritty, such as rising early or staying late to drive a delivery truck if need be. He doesn't mind. It's all for the good of the company.

Meanwhile, interesting things were happening back at the main Parmer company offices.

CHAPTER 4

"Every day, property/casualty insurers enable our economy to function by helping individuals and businesses address the various risks they face. In doing so, insurers take in premiums based on anticipated loss costs, keeping a small portion to cover operating expenses, and investing the rest until needed to pay claims or to hold aside to cover extraordinary losses.

"Thus, in addition to handling the risk of their policyholders and the larger society, insurance companies also have to be prudent and careful investors by managing the risk of the invested premium dollars. Because of the uncertainty and volatility of underwriting results, these investment returns can be a key source of financial stability for insurers in a competitive market.

"The industry's investment practices are geared towards being able to compensate policyholders quickly and efficiently, a business model that is also reinforced by statutory requirements."[14]

The insurance industry is highly regulated by the NAIC and subject to stiff investing guidelines. Large insurance companies with assets in the multiple billions of dollars usually handle premium investments in-house. Smaller companies with lower premium capital (although still in the multiple millions) hire external investment firms.

Covering three to four million homes across the nation,

---

14   http://www.aiadc.org/File%20Library/Member%20Center/Search%20Content/File%20
Upload/PD%20And%20R/2010/February/How%20PropertyCasualty%20Insurance%20
Companies%20Invest%20Premium%20Dollars%20(February%202010)-313776.pdf

RWC and its associated insurance entities Eastern Atlantic and Western Pacific handle millions of dollars of premium revenue that must be carefully monitored. According to industry regulations, 65% of these assets must be retained in cash and stable fixed income bonds. This is the portion that must be available to cover anticipated claims.

But some claims are not anticipated at all. For instance, Incurred But Not Reported (INBR) incidents can blindside an insurance company several years after they occur. Bob Yeselavage, director/treasurer/operations manager for Eastern Atlantic and WPMIC, notes one particular incident when 2014 INBR event wasn't presented for collection until 2016. An automobile turned into path of tractor trailer, causing three fatalities and two bad injuries. The survivors pursued payment from the truck insurer, but two years later they filed claims with the trailer owner, who happened to be insured by Eastern. Although the trailer had nothing to do with causing the injuries, Eastern was forced to pay. It was a totally unanticipated million-dollar loss for the company.

Eastern and WPMIC have reserves for those kinds of incidents. In fact, George routinely adds an additional 5-10% to recommended reserve amounts to be certain the funds will be there. He knows all too well that loss estimates can increase over time.

The other 35% of premium assets can be held in more speculative, but potentially more lucrative, financial securities. George has always followed his own conservative strategy for investing this portion of premium income. But the economic downturn and consequent skittishness in the stock market made him realize that perhaps he needed one or two more people to help him keep an eye on the company's growing portfolio.

Tom Seymour was brought on in 2007, at the very beginning of the downturn, to monitor certain segments of the market, assist with investment decisions, and handle trade transactions in specific areas. George instructed him with this directive on his first day, "The number one thing is to have fun. That is at the top of your job description."

That can sometimes be a tall order in a market that seems to defy logic. Stock indicators fluctuate wildly and trade decisions are often made without clear direction or concrete information. Tom has a little sign in his office that reads "Embrace Ambiguity." That's his mantra these days.

In 2013, George's son Adam graduated from Messiah College with a degree in Business and was hired to work alongside Tom as an Investment Analyst for the Parmer Companies. But that had not been his plan when he first entered college.

"I was really interested in history," he explains. But after his first year of college, he realized that the low credit requirements for a Business degree gave him a lot of flexibility to study a wide variety of disciplines. So, he took courses like Hebrew and audited other classes that interested him. His degree emphasized leadership skills – "soft skills" – that were enhanced by broad exposure to subjects not necessarily associated with business.

By his junior year, he was sporting a ponytail and wanted to be a philosopher, he laughs. Through Messiah's overseas program, he spent a semester in Israel at Jerusalem University College, surviving on pita bread and an "Arab version of Nutella." But he had many interesting and enlightening cross-cultural experiences and says enthusiastically, "I'd go back in a heartbeat."

He struggled after that, wondering if he really wanted to commit himself to his father's companies. He admits he didn't like the idea of "riding his father's coattails" and thought he should make his own way in the world. But he and his college advisor discussed that over a series of casual lunches and his advisor challenged Adam to examine his motives. Did his desire "be his own man" stem from a true calling, or was it a form of pridefulness? After some soul-searching, Adam realized that taking a role in the Parmer companies and carrying on his father's legacy was a unique God-given opportunity that should not be discarded.

Between his junior and senior year, he worked with Tom Seymour and suddenly realized that he really liked the investment side of the business.

"There's a lot of human behavior behind the market," he explains. "Rules don't always work." He realized that he could study all kinds of subjects and socio/political interactions as they affected the stock market. That appealed to his "philosopher side" and – voila! – he was hooked.

He recently created his own company within the Parmer collective. Enhancing Capital will be the asset management division that will guide and direct the investment funds of all the Parmer entities. "There's never been a proper advisor-client relationship between the companies and the internal investment team," he explains. They hired a Registered Investment Advisor to oversee and direct the company's compliance with government investment standards.

The new company will also handle investments for a limited number of private clients. Adam's plan is to develop a pooled fund that will function like a mutual fund, offering three investment strategies. He relishes the idea of building a variety of trading systems. To Adam, it is like a game or puzzle and appeals to his competitive streak. "There are a lot of ways to win," he says.

Most investments for the Parmer companies are long-term and "the biggest pieces just sit there," says Tom. These holdings churn consistent dividends that are reinvested, providing stability in a rapidly changing market. "[George] has to look at the financial world from many different perspectives," Tom reports. George views it from one angle, Adam looks at another, and Tom at a third. A fourth dimension is provided by a high-tech member of the team: a Bloomberg machine.

What in the world is a Bloomberg machine? "It's hard to communicate what it is," admits Tom. So let's turn to our old pal Wikipedia for a summary:

The Bloomberg Terminal is a computer software system provided by the financial data vendor Bloomberg L.P. that enables professionals in the financial service sector and other industries to access the Bloomberg Professional service through which users can monitor and analyze real-time financial market data and place trades on the electronic trading platform.[15] The system also provides news, price quotes, and messaging across its proprietary secure network. It is well-known among the financial community for its black interface, which is not optimized for user

---

15   "Bloomberg Professional." Bloomberg. Accessed at: https://www.bloomberg.com/professional/

experience but has become a recognizable trait of the service.[16,17]

So what does THAT mean? "A lot of info!" laughs Tom.

With a Bloomberg terminal, the RWC investment team can research any company for complex financial details. In addition to basic information about stock highs and lows for the year, number and kinds of employees, where companies are domiciled, current stock price, etc., links take the user deeper and deeper into company details, revealing complex charts, graphs, and visual projections. All of these are continually updated in real time, enabling users to follow any company's performance minute-by-minute.

It's almost like watching a baseball game in American Sign Language.

Twenty-nine analyst companies provide in-depth reviews about specific corporations and market sectors. They project how each company or industry, such as health, info-tech, pharmaceuticals, biotech, etc., is expected to perform within a specific time frame. Bloomberg informs investors if those sectors are weakening or strengthening, based on various indicators. If the investor wants further information, he is able to access numerous links to news articles and other related analyses.

Tom's job is to sift through the thousands of details to determine what is truly important for RWC's future investment decisions. He admits that it's easy to "go down bunny-trails" with so much information at his fingertips. Here's

---

16   Leca, Dominique. "The Impossible Bloomberg Makeover". UX. Accessed at: https://www.bloomberg.com/professional/
17   https://en.wikipedia.org/wiki/Bloomberg_Terminal#cite_note-1

where "embracing ambiguity" comes in. Data changes constantly and is influenced by dozens of interrelated factors, ranging from political and socio-economic conditions to the weather outlook. Analyst opinions always vary widely. So what's an investor to do?

The Parmer investment team uses many sophisticated trading methods to safeguard against losses in a fluctuating market. But what happens when a market sector truly looks like it's starting to tank? George, Tom, and Adam stay steady. It's the "Triple P Principle," explains Tom. "The Parmer Patience Principle." Plus an additional fourth P, in the negative – do NOT Panic! This philosophy has kept them safely strapped in the seat of many stock market roller-coasters over the years.

"As of October 2016, there were 325,000 Bloomberg Terminal subscribers worldwide."[18] For RWC warranty-holders or insurance clients, it's good to know that the Parmer Companies is one of them.

---

18   "Bloomberg company information". Bloomberg. Retrieved October 13, 2016. Accessed at: https://en.wikipedia.org/wiki/Bloomberg_Terminal#cite_note-1

George and Barbara Parmer

George and son Adam Parmer go over some plans.

Sisters Delores and Jean in their older days

George in his younger days...

George's mother and father, George J. and Mable M. Parmer

George's immediate family from left to right Son-in-Law Keith Dolon, Daughter Evie Dolon, grandson George Vincent Dolon, George, grandson Brady Dolon, wife Barbara Parmer, son Adam Parmer, daughter-in-law Hannah Parmer

Sister Delores, George, Cousin Leah Seaman, Sister Jean

Daughter Evie's wedding picture, from left to right, standing: George, son Adam Parmer, son-in-law Keith Dolon, son Carlin Brown, son-in-law Otis Cleveland. Sitting grandson Cooper Cleveland, grandson Max Cleveland, wife Barbara Parmer, daughter Evie Dolon, daughter Julia Davenport Cleveland, grandson Moses Cleveland

George's childhood home

Finding time for family life is very important to the Parmers. Here George and his wife Barbara are with two of their children, Adam and Evie.

George has supported several educational institutions, most recently as chairman of Messiah College's board.

George and son Adam on building site.

Headquarters of one of the Parmer companies, Fine Line Homes

Residential Warranty Company headquarters

All work and no play? That's not how it is at Parmer. Keeping things light is a vital part of running a successful family of companies.

From the start, the Parmer Corporation has prospered because of its people.

CHAPTER 5

"RWC recently held a luncheon to congratulate several Service Award recipients as well as to honor the years of stellar work from our four retirees: Rose Gibson, Betty Jane Zapf, Jim Haley and Don Sechler. Following a touching and amusing presentation by George Parmer, the retirees, their families and the rest of the Derry Street gang enjoyed a delicious catered meal capped off by assorted desserts and cake."[19]

This little snippet is only one of hundreds of similar articles spanning the years that the Parmer Companies have been in business. George has always encouraged and honored his staff with awards and luncheons. Good-natured contests have become highly-anticipated annual events. Nothing cut-throat, just friendly competition. Bonuses and promotions are distributed regularly and company parties, picnics, and other perks (three more Parmer "P's") are legendary.

Being an employee of any Parmer company is often described as like being a part of a big extended family. How does a business environment reach and maintain that level of comfort and fun-loving comraderie, while still maintaining a focused and efficient business environment?

"Employee engagement" is a vital factor in this dynamic. In an article entitled "Optimize" in the *Gallup Business*

---

19   "The Scoop" (company newsletter), Spring 2017.

Journal, authors John H. Fleming and Jim Harter explain:

> "Our research on employee engagement, based on feedback from more than 1.5 million workers, was path-breaking in demonstrating the supreme importance of human interactions to the bottom line. In order for employees to feel engaged, they must know what's expected of them, have the resources to do their jobs and get encouragement from bosses. They also need to feel they have opportunities to grow and that their opinions and ideas are taken seriously."[20]

This dynamic is exemplified in every Parmer company. For instance, general managers at each FLH location handle most decisions independently. Although the channels of communication with George are always open, he doesn't micro-manage anyone. Each location presents its own challenges and unique marketing niches. Local building codes vary, customer profiles and needs differ, and the areas are geographically diverse. He trusts that his managers and their staff have a far greater understanding of their territories and personnel than he does.

Senior VP Kathy Foley affirms that at RWC "most major decisions are discussed at length with all of the staff that has knowledge of or will be affected by the final outcome. Every voice – pro or con – is given equal consideration."

Parmer employees comment often about the egalitarian business environment at their workplaces. Says one, "No one is hung up on a person's job title." In fact, when asked to give their job titles, many Parmer employees have trou-

---

20   http://www.gallup.com/businessjournal/781/Optimize.aspx?g_source=Optimize&g_medium=search&g_campaign=tiles

ble defining them. Everyone does whatever he or she can to ensure success across the board for the entire Parmer corporate family. Says another, "We just sort of all move within this gel mass" like a giant amoeba. One manager explains, "I feel that my role is like a coach. I'm not a boss. My role is to allow employees to achieve their greatest potential."

One must be a team player with a teachable spirit to fit into the Parmer corporate environment. "I'll take attitude over aptitude any day," remarks one construction manager. "Many people came on board knowing literally nothing about the business, but having adaptable skills and the willingness to learn." Those are the employees he keeps. Past work experiences, even those unrelated to the building business, provide valuable input during decision-making and unusual employee backgrounds have become a source of strength. Parmer employees include a former day care worker, a hair stylist, a janitor, a reporter, a high school band director, and even one state congressional press secretary.

One skill set does especially well in the sales department. "Former athletes," notes Sue Palkovic, VP of Sales for RWC. "We have a football player, a tennis player, a basketball player." She always asks about their outside activities in an interview and if they've been an athlete, she knows they will excel at Parmer company contests and competing for special perks.

A strong work ethic permeates the companies, but it's not the primary focus. Explains Kathy Foley, "We will not be remembered for how well we handled our workloads, but rather by how well we treated our co-workers, friends, and family. To do unto others as you would have them do unto you."[21]

John Schilling, current IT manager, describes the life/work balance this way. "It's a triangle," he says, "Family, faith, work. They all interact. If all the angles of the triangle are equal, you have a good life." George wants his employees to maintain that "tripod balance." In fact, says John, he once upset George by continually staying too late at the office and being a bit too conscientious about certain aspects of his job. George clearly expressed his disapproval and John laughs, "I was on George's wrong side and that's not a good place to be!"

The current trend in our culture is for professionals to move from one company to another in order to advance in their careers. But the Parmer corporations are counter-cultural in this respect. Says John Kerschner, "If you're young and ambitious and have talent, there are growth positions within the companies." A large number of employees stay long-term and have moved up through the ranks. George muses about their commitment, "Some people might think 'Wow, he must be a good guy to have people working for him for 30 years.' I don't look at it like that. I look at it that they gave up 30 years to help this company get to where it is. I don't take it lightly." In a March, 1997, interview with the *Sunday Patriot News*, George remarked, "If this were a baseball team, I wouldn't trade any of them because I would win the World Series every time out with this team." He still feels that way 21 years later.

In 2014, the average tenure of an employee at RWC was 18 years, the Warranty Resolution staff average was 17 years, and the management team average was 27.5 years.

---

21   Matthew 7:12

"[George] generates loyalty among his employees," one manager explains. "[It's] a two-way street. George is loyal to his people and his people are loyal to him."

Remember the story about the retirement plans? That was one example of how George provides benefits to his employees that will affect their families as well. In a Forbes article entitled "The Secret of Employee Engagement Isn't About Your Employees," writer Ryan Westwood explains,

"Here's what I've found: If you want a great culture and true employee engagement, provide benefits that positively impact not just your employees but, more importantly, those whom they love. Employees go home to different roles – parent, caregiver to a loved one, a church or civic leader, spouse, bandmate, freelancer, artist, neighbor – and the people they are closest to impact their lives and perspectives about work in meaningful ways."[22]

Westwood's three keys to employee engagement are:

- Focus on health insurance.

- Make sure company parties reflect the work culture.

- Remember: gifts go a long way.

Intuitively, George has nailed all three.

His commitment to the welfare of his employees has inspired some decisions in the past that were not necessarily the most profitable for him personally. Years ago, a Fortune 500 company was interested in purchasing parts of his busi-

---

22   https://www.forbes.com/sites/ryanwestwood/2017/10/30/the-secret-to-employee-engagement-isnt-about-your-employees/#2413dcef1ed4

ness. George would continue to run it for them for the first five years and report to their headquarters every quarter. It was a lucrative deal, but meant that George would lose control over most major decisions directly impacting his employees. That made him uneasy and after careful consideration, although it was a good financial deal, he decided not to sell.

This was not the only time he's been approached with an offer to be bought out. In fact, he reports that he receives inquiries once per week, on average. He turns them all down.

George's loyalty to his staff is reflected in their loyalty to one another. Kathy Foley explains, "The company allows employees to donate earned, unused leave time to employees who have exhausted their own personal leave due to medical problems experienced by [that] employee or [one of his or her] family members." This inter-staff generosity, plus a benevolence fund that George created, has eased many employee hardships over the years.

Sometimes, as with any family, disputes occur. "This is a quirky little family," laughs Sue Palkovic. "There are times you want to punch your brother in the nose and other times you want to give him a hug. That's the way it is around here." But, she adds quickly, there are "more hugs than punches!"

Of course, the punches are rhetorical. Interoffice disputes are handled quickly and efficiently. At RWC, Kathy Foley oversees the process. If disagreements turn into true grievances, she becomes the designated arbiter, investigating the grievance and providing written findings to the offended employee. The other Parmer entities follow similar protocols. By being proactive, managers prevent staff concerns from becoming festering sores that infect and poison the corporate atmosphere.

This dynamic is a direct reflection of George's personal leadership style. One employee muses that George's presence "fills a room." What is that intangible quality? In her book, *Leading with Y.E.S.*, leadership coach Maria van Hekken describes it this way.

"Leadership is the ability to inspire others to want to achieve a common vision and presence. Sometimes when you meet a person, you get an intangible sense of inspiration. It's reflected in this formula: leadership + presence = the quality that inspires people to achieve a common vision. What's more, positive leadership presence takes everything to the next level, inspires people to imagine new possibilities, and encourages them to utilize their strengths to accomplish their shared vision."[23]

In addition, she notes that "trust, caring, and being real... are three fundamental prerequisites for positive leadership presence."

Adam had his father take the Clifton Strengths Finder[24] assessment and the results revealed that George is a "maximizer," someone who excels at seeing the big picture, diagnosing problems, and finding solutions. Rather than dictating courses of action, maximizers lead others to consider

---

23   vanHekken, Maria. *Leading with Y.E.S.* 2017. YestoYes Insights, Allentown, PA, unpaginated digital edition. https://www.amazon.com/Leading-S-Practical-Discovering-Extraordinary-ebook/dp/B0745K8JBW/ref=sr_1_1?ie=UTF8&qid=1510323596&sr=8-1&keywords=leading+with+yes

24   https://www.gallupstrengthscenter.com/?utm_source=google&utm_medium=cpc&utm_campaign=Strengths_ECommerce_Brand_Search_US&utm_content=gallup%2strengthsfinder&gclid=CjwKCAjwypjVBRANEiwAJAxlIhSDZrLGQ81j1VcgDFDn_iGpaw8yM-mCRBDxZYwlBh4OEU0KURTcExoClfQQAvD_BwE

various options and come up with reasonable strategies on their own. George instinctually cycles through a series of thoughtful management behaviors as he interacts with managers and associates. Adam admits that although he understands this ability, it's not as second-nature to him as it is to George. But he's watching and learning every day.

Many organizations have recognized these qualities in George and he has been tapped to serve on several boards of directors. In 1998, he became a director at Fulton Bank, a position he held through 2012. He would have stayed on longer, but the bank rules mandated director retirement at 72.

Not so for Sunshine Bank in Florida. George's age wasn't a problem for them and they quickly snatched him up for their board. During his tenure, the bank increased its assets from $200 million to over $1 billion. He will finally relinquish his position this year as the Sunshine board dissolves in acquisition by another entity. Says George, "As a board member, you do your best for the shareholders. That's who you work for." For Sunshine shareholders, the sale is a good deal.

Also in the late '90s, George was elected to the board of Messiah College in Grantham, PA. It's a large, diverse board of over 30 directors. "They all have different gifts. These are not lightweights. One is the CFO of T. Rowe Price. One is the owner of Martin's Potato Rolls. To me it's mind-boggling. I'm now the board chair. What am I doing there? My profile says I shouldn't be doing that. But here I am. I don't know how to answer that. God has been so gracious to me."

Trustees of Messiah typically serve for nine years and

then must take a year off. But when George's ninth year approached, the college made him a "lifelong member," effectively cancelling his furlough year. He is now the board chair. He marvels at the cooperative dynamic on that board. "There's never a fight," he says. "We do the best for the college, whatever that is. We have a lot of discussion. If they don't use my idea, I don't get excited about it." When he calls for a vote, he says, the response is always unanimous.

In 2010, he got a call from the owner of Four Seasons Produce in Ephrata who was forming a board for his business and wanted George to be a director. "Why did you pick me?" he asked. He was told that the owner knew a Messiah trustee who had recommended him. Four board members currently serve. One is the ex-CEO of Giant Foods, one is CEO of IGA, and another was the produce provider for Sam's Clubs national-wide. "I have no idea what I'm doing there!" George says with a laugh. But then he adds, "I'm always questioning costs, so I keep them fiscally tight." During his tenure, Four Seasons has "grown amazingly" in the last seven years.

This book isn't long enough to cite all of the philanthropic activity of the Parmer family, both personally and through their Parmer Family Foundation. The majority is for Christian causes: Messiah College, Harrisburg Christian School, Covenant Christian Academy, and the like. "We just want more and more people to come to know Christ." Son Adam agrees. "We like to be generous, but we want our giving to be in line with what we want to accomplish."

Suffice it to say that Central Penn Business Journal recognized this in 2015 by awarding George its Philanthropist of the Year award. The awards ceremony was hard for him.

"I don't particularly like the recognition," he admits. But, reports Barbara, "his family really enjoyed a formal evening out – all dressed up!"

Adam recognizes that awards like that put "a big target" on his father's back. Growing up with wealth comes with its own unique challenges. Adam has always been very cautious about keeping his family's wealth under wraps as much as he is able. For example, he never brought a date to his home (with the exception of Hannah, the girl he married.) "The last thing I wanted was for [a date] to see the dollar signs." He admits that it is hard sometimes to determine exactly why a person or organization is approaching him for friendship or leadership. But he's learning how to ferret out the genuine from the opportunistic.

His father George admits that at one time he idolized money. "I was so poor for so long that I thought it was the avenue to everything. I realize now that that was dead wrong." He controls assets in the multi-millions and his focus now is "to be a good steward of them."

Stewardship is not a random idea. It is a result of the wisdom he has acquired in the years since he became a Christian in the early 1990s. He remembers the night he first felt the call to come to the Lord.

It was during the time when he and Betty decided to end their marriage. One evening he drove to the office in the middle of the night. "I remember praying," he says, but doesn't remember the details. "I wasn't really good at that at that point." But afterwards he says he felt a peace that he never felt before and that he can't explain. "I wasn't even sure how to come to the Lord," he admits. But soon afterwards, he found out about the sinner's prayer – confession and repentance – and accepting Jesus Christ as his personal savior. That "was pretty easy," he says. When he took that formal step, he thinks he was "already saved, but just didn't know it."

His conversion to Christianity reshaped George's desires and his future. Before he was a Christian, he used a lot of bad language. "I was the biggest cusser around. In construction, everyone uses bad language." But he admits he was the best – or worst – of them. When he became a Christian "I just stopped," he says. The change was dramatic and immediately noticed by all of his employees and business associates.

He vowed never to swear again, but had one brief violation that humbled him. While giving a deposition to an attorney in a lawsuit ("one of the nastiest attorneys you'd ever want to meet," he notes), George became really angry and he let loose with some cuss words that he hadn't uttered in over two years. He stopped abruptly, got up, and stood in the corner of the room. "That guy probably thought I was a nut case," he says. George's eyes teared up and he said aloud, "Lord, forgive me." The attorney looked at him like he was crazy, but George didn't care. "I had broken a vow." It was a powerful and emotional moment for him.

That vow is embodied in a faded card that he keeps on his desk. It is a "Righteousness Pledge" of personal integrity that he signed in 1995, shortly after he and Barbara began attending Trinity Presbyterian Church. They had just moved into their Grove Road home and Trinity was close by. After visiting three or four times, he asked Barbara and his mother-in-law Doris, who was living with them, if they wanted to try any other churches. "No. Why would we do that?" Doris asked. They became members and have been there ever since. Trinity soon recognized George's leadership talent and he was ordained as an elder in the early 2000s. He's been serving in that capacity for over 15 years.

Unlike their own upbringings, George and Barbara raised their son Adam and daughter Eve in a Christian home that embraced most of the child-raising boundaries established by other families in their church. Although Adam remembers being given a great deal of freedom as a teenager, that did not include permission to work anywhere but at a Parmer company. He admits he would have loved to have worked at a "horrible place" – like a store at the mall or a fast food restaurant – just to have the experiences his father did, but George and Barbara always nixed those ideas. He understands his parents' reasons for that decision, but he thinks he will allow his own teenaged children to get typical summer jobs outside of the Parmer companies.

George and Barbara taught Adam and Eve to appreciate what they had and always work hard. When an employee recently asked Adam why he didn't drive a Tesla, he told him that he just didn't need one. Just because he *can* have one doesn't mean he *should* have one.

In addition to instilling Biblical principles at home, George started a Bible study at RWC headquarters that meets early every Wednesday morning. It is open to all and has been going strong for 20 years. He is also a member of the Gideons International, an organization that distributes free Bibles and New Testaments throughout the world.[25] George believes in planting "Good News seeds"[26] wherever he can. Years ago, he gave one of these New Testaments to a non-believer who briefly attended his Bible study. The little book was found among the young man's possessions after his untimely death in a traffic accident. Opening it, the young man's father – a FLH employee – noticed with joy and relief that his son had signed and dated the commitment page in the back. He had become a believer by reading that tiny New Testament.

"When I look back, I feel that the Lord was shaping me and teaching me. I've been through the bad times. I shouldn't be where I am today. I didn't go to college. I was a goof-off in high school. I wanted to be a truck driver. What the heck am I doing here? It has to be Him. It's not me. I give all the glory to the Lord. Somehow, He steered me through. A lot of times I shouldn't have made it. But God puts people in your path. I can give you example after example."

Does he consider his business a ministry? "That's a good question," he muses.

"I'm hopeful that he's given me these assets to help, as a means to grow the Kingdom." He hopes this will continue after he goes to be with the Lord. To guide the corporate vision, he assembled a board of trustees with key leaders from within his companies. "I'm slightly stepping back," he says. "When I came into this world I had nothing. When I leave I'll have nothing."

---

25   https://www2.gideons.org
26   Matthew 13: 1-23

As a vice-president and "heir-apparent" of the companies, Adam embraces his role as a servant-leader. He likes to be stretched and challenged and would love to go to graduate school someday, perhaps in a different academic discipline. But for the time being, his goal is to add "his layer of bricks" onto the foundation his father built. Some managers have hinted to Adam that he might want to replace all of them when he is in charge, but that's the farthest thing from his mind. He knows the value of good people. "If I did that I'd have huge problems!" he laughs.

What is the one thing George would have done differently? The answer comes quickly: "I'd have come to the Lord at an earlier age!" His greatest joy, of course, is his family. "Nothing is more satisfying to me than that they follow the Lord." When he bows his head while grandsons Brady or Vince pray before a meal, he is full of gratitude. "How can that not be pleasing to a grandparent? That's a blessing!"

Someday, Lord willing, those grandchildren will be adding their own chapters to this book.

Made in the USA
Middletown, DE
20 May 2022

66010048R00046